Twitter:

Jack Dorsey, Biz Stone and Evan Williams

Twitter:
Jack Dorsey, Biz Stone and Evan Williams

Chris Smith
and Marci McGrath

Greensboro, North Carolina

To Rebecca, Jason, Sarah, and Jeff—
our favorite social network.

twitter™

See what people are saying about...

anyone wanna be my friend?|

POPULAR TOPIC

New Moon   Follow Friday   TGIF

27   New Moon   #openwebawards   #FunnyButN

New Moon   #theresway2many   Modern Warfare 2

© 2009 Twitter   About Us   Contact   Blog   Status   Goodies

ws (369) ▾   MySpace

Twitter home page

Twitter

Share and discover what's happening right now, anywhere in the world

Search

Sign up now

prah #newmoon Google Chrome OS

Cool #nottosayonfirstdate

umightbealiberal

Business

Business Leaders

Twitter: Jack Dorsey, Biz Stone and Evan Williams
Copyright © 2012 by Morgan Reynolds Publishing

Morgan Reynolds Publishing, Inc.
620 South Elm Street, Suite 387
Greensboro, NC 27406 USA

Library of Congress Cataloging-in-Publication Data

Smith, Chris.
 Business leaders : Twitter : Jack Dorsey, Biz Stone and Evan Williams /
by Chris Smith and Marci McGrath.
     p. cm.
Includes bibliographical references and index.
ISBN 978-1-59935-179-7 -- ISBN 978-1-59935-216-9 (e-book)
1. Twitter--Juvenile literature. 2. Instant messaging--Juvenile
literature. 3. Internet--Social aspects--Juvenile literature. 4. Dorsey,
Jack, 1976- 5. Williams, Evan, 1972- 6. Stone, Biz. I. McGrath, Marci.
II. Title.
 HM743.T95S65 2012
 006.7092'273--dc23
 [B]
                          2011024699

Printed in the United States of America
First Edition

Book cover and interior designed by:
Ed Morgan, navyblue design studio
Greensboro, NC

Table of Contents

Chapter 1

What is Twitter?

The Magic of Maps

Twitter was born during a brainstorming session. Employees at a San Francisco podcasting company called Odeo had gathered in a city park and broken into groups to come up with ideas. Jack Dorsey, a young software engineer and relatively new hire, was perched atop a playground slide. He suggested a simple way to send status updates by using text messages—an idea Jack had been fiddling with for years. "I was lucky enough to be in @Jack's group," Odeo's Dom Sagolla later recalled in a blog, "where he first described a service that uses SMS [Short Message Service] to tell small groups what you are doing. It was sunny and brisk. We were eating Mexican food. His idea made us stop eating and start talking."

Odeo's co-founder, Evan Williams, liked Dorsey's idea and so did Biz Stone, the company's creative director. Stone and Dorsey produced a Twitter prototype in two weeks and implemented it as an internal service for Odeo employees. "The first version of @Jack's idea was entirely web-based," said Sagolla. "It was created on March 21st, 2006."

A full version of the service launched a few months later. Then in April 2007, Twitter was spun off as a company separate from Odeo, with Jack serving as its first chief executive, Biz as creative director, and Ev, short for Evan, as chairman.

What started as a way for friends to communicate with each other, in messages of no more than 140 characters, has evolved into a social phenomenon. Twitter's nearly 200 million users post more than 1 billion tweets weekly, on everything from natural disasters like the earthquake in Japan to updates on protests sweeping the Arab world. Said Stone: "Twitter is the side project that took."

In some ways, Ev, Biz, and Jack couldn't be more different—one grew up on a Nebraska farm, another in a suburb in New England, and the other in a city in middle America. But they also share some common characteristics: each attended a university, or two, for a while, but

Twitter co-founders (from left) Evan Williams, Biz Stone, and Jack Dorsey in their offices in downtown San Francisco

quit—distracted by their own individual pursuits and the need to be independent. And each could easily be described as serial start-up entrepreneurs.

Odeo's Evan Williams grew up on a soybean, corn, and cattle farm near Clarks, Nebraska—population 361. The public school he attended—there was only one in the town—had fourteen students. Christopher Isaac "Biz" Stone was raised in Wellesley, Massachusetts. Like Jack and Ev, Biz showed an interest at an early age in starting things and leading people. When his high school didn't have a lacrosse team, Biz started one. When the school's senior play was canceled, he led other students in producing one anyway.

Jack Dorsey was born in St. Louis, Missouri, on November 19, 1976. Before he became known as the

A view of downtown St. Louis from the Gateway Arch

inventor of Twitter, he was just a boy in St. Louis who couldn't learn enough about cities and maps, and how people get packages from one place to another. "Since I was very small, I've been fascinated by how cities work," he said. "I always got really excited when I thought about visualizing them, specifically around maps. What would you place on a map to show how a city worked?"

Jack's parents, Tim and Marcia Dorsey, moved to several other cities in Missouri and Colorado while raising Jack and his brothers, Dan and Andrew. Early in Jack's life, his family realized he had a strong imagination and the ambition to use it in business. Tim Dorsey recalled that Jack "was really creative as a child. He has that right brain/left brain thing going. He's creative and analytical at the same time."

By the age of fourteen, Jack began to spend countless hours walking around downtown St. Louis, watching how vehicles and people moved. He and his younger brother Danny were fascinated by trains too. They took a video camera to the railroad tracks just to record a moving train. But cars and other street vehicles were by far the most interesting to Jack. Intersections, he felt, were especially appealing, because that was where people came together briefly before they moved on to wherever they were going.

Jack decided to teach himself to write software code so he could create maps and show movement on a computer. It wasn't long before that skill helped him find a job that would let him develop his talent. In a way, the job found Jack. An employee of Mira Digital Publishing, a software company in St. Louis, walked into a coffee shop that just happened to be owned by Jack's mother. While drinking his coffee the man said that he had an urgent need to hire programmers. Marcia Dorsey said, "My son loves computers."

That was that. The company hired Jack Dorsey, then fifteen, as a summer intern. The owner, Jack McKelvey, was busy running his growing business, but it didn't take long for Jack Dorsey to make an impression. One day McKelvey was busy working at his computer, entering data, and his new employee introduced himself.

"I'll be with you in a minute," McKelvey said. But he kept working and eventually forgot Jack was standing there. When McKelvey stood up to take a break from his computer, he was surprised to see that Jack Dorsey was still standing there.

"Jack was in exactly the same position. He'd been motionless for 45 minutes," McKelvey remembered. Before long, he realized that the young man was able to do more for the software company than run errands and simple computer tasks. McKelvey heard Jack say that

Mira Digital Publishing should start thinking about doing business on the Internet, something that didn't seem to interest the other employees. McKelvey took a chance. He put Jack Dorsey in charge of the Internet project and hired several other programmers to help him. "Just do everything this kid says," McKelvey instructed his employees.

The teenager showed he had a knack for managing people. McKelvey later said only half-jokingly: "I was the president of the company and he was the summer intern. But that doesn't necessarily mean I wasn't the one running errands."

As glad as Jack was to be working, he was already looking for a way to become his own boss so he could work full-time on computerized map programming. He wanted to create software to handle the dispatch of couriers. Since he didn't know anyone at a courier company in St. Louis, he talked his brother into starting their own bike courier service.

Although the Dorseys' new business was a flop at finding customers, the experience gave Jack good practice at using a computer to map information. So good, it later turned out, that some open source software—software that is free for anyone else to use or to improve as they see fit—written by Jack while he was a teenager is still used by some taxicab companies.

In school, Jack was not a student who stood out. In fact, many childhood friends and teachers describe Jack— if they remember him at all—as quiet most of the time.

He was not what you would call socially popular. If you wanted to get him to perk up and start talking, the trick was to bring up the subject of computers, or the Internet, which wasn't widely known at the time.

After high school, Jack enrolled at the University of Missouri at Rolla, which is just over one hundred miles west of St. Louis. His parents wanted him to stay close to home. The university, later renamed Missouri University of Science and Technology, had a technology program that must have appealed to him.

At first, Jack Dorsey liked college life in Rolla, Missouri. It seemed like a good next step for someone in a hurry to learn more about computers and put that knowledge to work in business. Between classes, he practiced his hobby of writing software for dispatching ambulances and couriers. But no matter how much he

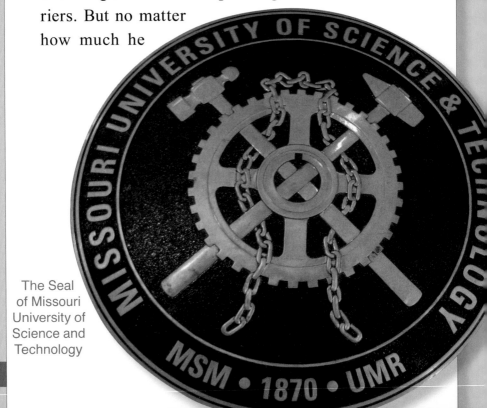

The Seal of Missouri University of Science and Technology

enjoyed college life away from home, he couldn't help thinking that a small city in the middle of Missouri was no match for the busy streets of a big, bustling city. After a couple of semesters at Rolla, Jack started to wonder what it would be like to live and work in a large city on the East or West coast, where important companies were based and millions of people pursued their dreams.

Should he go west, to join the booming technology industry in Silicon Valley, near San Francisco? The research labs there were full of ideas that led to new products such as laser printers and new graphical screens on personal computers. Famous people including Bill Gates of Microsoft and Steve Jobs of Apple had started their business empires on the West Coast; maybe Jack could follow their example. Silicon Valley had thousands of other young people working on their computer ideas. That was tempting.

Or should he go east, to New York, to see if the real city matched the excitement he had imagined as a child? New York had countless thousands of people and vehicles, constantly moving around on a network of streets unlike anything on earth. Think of the computerized maps he could create.

It was a tough choice, but in the end Jack's love for the world of dispatch technology helped him decide. During his junior year in college at Rolla, one day he found the Web site of Dispatch Management Services Corporation, or DMSC, a successful company in New York that was

Jack Dorsey

well-known for creating dispatch systems for couriers in the city. The idea of writing software that directed messengers around New York City on foot, or on two or four wheels, was too much to resist.

Using his computer skills, Jack combed through every corner of DMSC's Web site and found the e-mail address of its founder, Greg Kidd. He also managed to get access to other pages on the Web site that he was pretty sure shouldn't have been available to anyone outside the company. To introduce himself, Jack e-mailed Kidd to tell him about the security hole he had found in the DMSC Web site, and gave Kidd advice on how to fix it. Oh, and by the way, Jack added, I know how to write dispatch software too.

Greg Kidd was so amazed by the skill and attitude of this young, unknown programmer from Missouri that he called Jack on the phone and offered him a job. With little hesitation, Jack said yes. He broke the news to his family and college friends in Missouri, and applied for an academic transfer to New York University (NYU). Within two weeks of contacting Greg Kidd, Jack moved to the Big Apple, and the New York move would soon put him on a path leading to Ev and Biz.

twitter

Chapter 2

What is Twitter?

East Coast, West Coast

Evan Williams was born March 31, 1972, and grew up on a farm "90 miles and an eternity" from Lincoln, Nebraska. He liked to check out books on Babe Ruth and dinosaurs at the local library in his small farm community.

Even as a young boy, Ev said he had "a fierce desire to create things, to be independent and prove myself, which caused me to reject authority, but never in a rebellious way. It was more like, 'I'm going to show you by doing it all myself.'"

Evan Williams at the 2001 Webby Awards

In his senior year of high school, Ev moved to Columbus, Nebraska, and graduated from Columbus High School in 1990. After high school, he attended the University of Nebraska for a year-and-a-half before dropping out. "I felt college was a waste of time; I wanted to start working. I moved to Florida, where I did some freelance copy writing. After that I moved to Texas and stayed with my older sister while I figured out what to do next. In 1994, I returned to Nebraska and started my first company with my dad."

Ev, his dad, and friends began producing CD-ROMs and a video on how to use the Internet. They also did Web hosting. However, none of them knew how to write software, and with little money to keep the start-up going, the business shut down. He later said:

I had no business running a company at that time because I hadn't worked at a real company. I didn't know how to deal with people, I lacked focus, and I had no discipline. I'd start new projects without finishing old ones, and I didn't keep track of money. I lost a lot of it, including what my father had invested, and I ended up owing the I.R.S. because I hadn't paid payroll taxes. I made a lot of employees mad.

In 1999, Ev moved to California to work at O'Reilly Media. "I was lucky O'Reilly took a chance on me, especially because I wasn't particularly good at the job," he says. "I got a salary of $48,500. However, I had over $10k in credit-card debt, plus student loans, so I was barely paying my new California-style rent at that rate."

It wasn't long before Ev got frustrated with the job and quit—after seven months. He didn't like working for other people and couldn't resist the urge to start his own company. So he and his then girlfriend, Meg Hourihan, founded a software company called Pyra Labs, which created Blogger.com, one of the first Internet services that let anyone create an online journal known as a weblog. There, they could publish their own words, pictures or other content online. Ev Williams soon started calling weblogs "blogs" for short. He may have been the first person to use the term "blogger" for those who wrote blogs.

Meanwhile, Biz Stone was charting his own course. Born on March 10, 1974, in Boston, Massachusetts, he grew up in nearby Wellesley. His parents divorced when he was still young, and he says he never had a "real relationship" with his father, a mechanic with a Boston accent. His mother was an assistant teacher at his elementary school, and Biz says he got teased because of that. Though it could be assumed that the name "Biz" might have something to do with business, it's actually a nickname he acquired as a small boy. Biz couldn't pronounce his name. Instead of saying Christopher, he pronounced it as "Bizober." By the time he was in the third grade, nobody called him anything other than "Biz."

Biz Stone

At Wellesley High School, Biz produced and starred in a production of Robin Hood, which turned out to be more comical than dramatic. He also tried out for all of the school's sports teams, but didn't make one. He didn't give up, though. He talked school administrators into setting up a lacrosse team, which the school didn't have at the time. "It turned out that I was really good at lacrosse," he said, "the others elected me captain, and we were a good team."

Biz learned a lesson from the experience that he's never forgotten:

> Opportunity can be manufactured. Yes, you can wait around for the right set of circumstances to fall into place and then leap into action, but you can also create those set of circumstances on your own. In doing so, you manufacture your own opportunities. This is as true for high school sports as it is for entrepreneurism or corporate culture. It has helped me immeasurably.

After high school, Biz studied writing at Northeastern University and the arts at the University of Massachusetts but dropped out of both universities after one year. He had a student job with the publisher Little, Brown, moving boxes, but got a promotion to full-time graphic designer after sneaking his book jacket designs into the art department's files.

In 1999 Biz and a friend started Xanga.com, a blogging Web site. He built a reputation as an expert in blogs, and even wrote a book on the subject. But he left Xanga soon after helping to found it.

Xanga, the blogging community Web site

Evan Williams had been an admirer of Biz's work and invited him to join Blogger. Biz jumped at the chance and moved West to take the job. But in 2003 the fast-growing Internet search company Google bought Pyra Labs, one of many creative companies that Google bought in order to offer new technology features to its customers.

Both Ev and Biz became Google employees. Twenty months later, however, the duo left Google to start their own company, Odeo.

Earlier, around the time Ev Williams moved to California and began his career as a computer programmer, Jack Dorsey was getting started in New York. The dispatch software business at DMSC was going well, but Jack and Greg Kidd thought they could make it even better. The best place to do that, they believed, was in California, where there were more dollars, people, and computers for building new technology.

This time, Jack decided to put his formal education on hold instead of transferring to another college. His parents were worried about him dropping out of NYU, but they realized that their son was determined to work full-time toward his dreams. Besides, they thought, anyone as smart as Jack Dorsey can easily go back to college and get his degree later.

Although he was only a semester short of graduating, in 1998 Jack dropped out of school and bought a ticket to San Francisco. There, he and Greg Kidd founded a new company, dNET, short for Dispatch Network. By that time the Internet was becoming a booming place for business, and they wanted to build an online system that companies would use to keep track of their couriers and pay them. A group of computer investors in California known as the Band of Angels liked the idea enough to give Greg and Jack money to get started. That kind of investment in a new company, known as venture capital, or "seed money," is a key part of keeping technology businesses going until they can make a product and sell it.

As soon as Greg Kidd and Jack Dorsey had money from their investors, they hired a chief executive officer (CEO) to run the business so they could focus on writing software and managing several other young programmers they had hired. Things were looking good. But the frenzy of investments in hundreds of new high-tech companies like dNET during the late 1990s had gone too far. When the price of technology stocks dropped rapidly in the market, many of those companies that weren't yet making any money were suddenly in big trouble. To make things worse, the CEO they had hired to take care of business disagreed with Greg and Jack and, since the CEO was in charge, he fired both of them. They had started the company, but now they were out of a job.

It wasn't the first time Jack had been part of a business failure—the Dorsey brothers' bike courier company had gone bust too—but the bursting of the "dot-com bubble" was the first grownup shock in Jack Dorsey's career. He hung around the Bay Area for a while, but the prospects for a computer job there were poor at the time. Hundreds of other young programmers were out of work too. Jack Dorsey's journey to the East Coast, then the West Coast, had been exciting. However, for the moment, he was right back where he started: unemployed and unsure how to use his great ideas to build a career. Always logical, in 2002 Jack packed his bags and headed home, to St. Louis.

There, he worked for his father while he figured out what to do with his life. Jack thought briefly about turning his drawing hobby into a career. It wasn't the same as programming, but drawing illustrations of flowers would at least keep him close to two things he loved: science and artistic design. While still in St. Louis, he considered another potential career, massage therapy, when he got massage treatment for a wrist injury. Jack completed formal training and got his certification as a massage therapist.

Eventually, Jack felt the call of the West again, so he took his newfound skills back to San Francisco. He moved into a small room in the backyard of his friend and former business partner Greg Kidd. Unable to find much work as a massage therapist, Jack took a series of other jobs in the city just to survive. He even served as a nanny for Kidd's daughter for a while. Eventually, his software skills landed Jack some temporary work. One program he wrote is still used to sell and print tickets to tour Alcatraz Island. Encouraged by the work, Jack began to look for a full-time programming job again. The technology industry was recovering from the dot-com bust, and Jack heard that a new company, Odeo, needed a programmer.

For the first time in his life, Jack created a written resume—just a simple list of the jobs he had already held—and sent it to Odeo. The company hired him for

Evan Williams, co-founder and CEO of Odeo, poses with a screen showing his company's site at his offices in San Francisco in 2005.

a few weeks on a trial basis. His new boss was Evan Williams. Jack's daily work at Odeo was nothing like the dispatch programming that had taken him from Missouri to New York to San Francisco. Instead, Jack was working on software that helped people download podcast recordings for playback on their computers or MP3 players. No more mapping of the movement of people around a city, or their constant back-and-forth communication about where they were and what they were doing. At least he was making money again as a computer programmer.

Soon, Jack and his new friends at Odeo would face a big threat to their business, but would also discover that one of his old ideas had the potential to change everything about how people communicated on the Internet.

Chapter 3

What is Twitter?

Setting Up Twitter

Now that he had a software career again, Jack Dorsey's life in San Francisco was looking up. Hair in dreadlocks, rings in his ears and nose, he had his own sense of personal style that didn't always fit with the ideas of employers. The nose ring nearly got him fired from one part-time job.

Jack also kept up his interest in designing things other than software. Clothing design appealed to him. Once again, as with massage therapy, when Jack wanted to learn more, he enrolled in classes at a trade school, this time studying how to design and sew clothing. Not content just to wear jeans, he wanted to make his own.

"I was fascinated with jeans because you can impress your life upon the jeans you wear," he said. Jack applied his fascination with patterns to his new subject, and kept studying and practicing basic clothing design for a while. Soon, however, big developments would take him away from fashion before he had a chance to make his own jeans.

The job at Odeo was going fine and Jack's programming skills convinced the company to keep him employed. He was enjoying the chance to work with other young, energetic entrepreneurs like Evan and Biz.

Jack had never let go of his childhood interest in mapping people's activity. From his work as a summer intern, to his and his brother's bicycle delivery business, to programming for DMSC in New York, and on to California, Jack kept working on a simple idea: how could computers be used to tell a person's status at any given time?

He tried to get friends interested in the idea in 2000, when he and Greg Kidd were working at dNet. Jack had been one of the first people he knew to buy a portable e-mail device, the RIM 850. It was made by the company that would later produce the BlackBerry. At a point when most people were happy just to have a cell phone, or were excited about the chance to have their calendar and other

The RIM 850

information in their phone, Jack wanted to do more with the new portable gadget.

He and his friends were starting to use instant messaging on the Internet too. Again, while others were content to use their "buddy list" of contacts and IM from their computers to send messages to one person at a time, Jack got creative. What if, instead of having to sit at your computer and send instant messages, you could use your cell phone to IM a group of people anytime and anywhere you felt like it? He remembered what happened next: "One night, I couldn't sleep, I just had to write a prototype script. It would sit on a server, take incoming e-mails, broadcast them out to a list, and also record them in a database that I could view on the Web."

To try out his new brainstorm, Jack put five of his friends' e-mail addresses into the new program, grabbed his portable e-mail device and went for a walk in San Francisco's Golden Gate Park. It was time to test his idea in real life. He pulled the RIM out of his pocket, typed an e-mail message that read, "I'm at the Bison Paddock watching the bison," and hit Send. Then he waited. And waited. Apparently, this instant status-update idea would only make sense if the five friends all had a mobile e-mail device too. None of them did, so unless they happened to be sitting at a computer checking e-mail when Jack was in the park, there was nothing "instant" about the new messages at all.

Jack later laughed and added that "secondly, no one really cared what I was doing in the park."

But at the time he felt that, just because other people weren't ready for the idea, it didn't mean it wasn't an idea worth keeping. He kept working on the programming and even gave it a name in 2001: Stat.us.

Jack and the rest of the young programming team at Odeo were working hard on other projects. But just as with dNet and the dot-com bust a few years before, things were not always within Jack's or his company's control. Odeo had planned for its most important product to be an online directory of podcasts. Customers would log on, search for recordings of interest, and download or

Bison at San Francisco's Golden Gate Park, where Jack was when he sent the first mass IM

subscribe to them. At the time, Apple's iTunes service was fairly new, and then it was focused mostly on song recordings.

But when Apple added podcasts to iTunes in June 2005, it meant big trouble for Odeo and other companies that were competing to sell podcast software. Within a few months, it was clear that the young company would go

Steve Jobs, Apple's CEO, on stage at the launch of Apple's iTunes music store in London in 2004

broke unless it could find a different product to make and sell. Ev Williams told everyone at Odeo to brainstorm ideas that might be worth developing.

Jack wondered if his idea for e-mail status updates might be the answer, but he remembered how few people had been interested in that one. Fortunately, another type of communication was then becoming popular among cell phone users in the United States: text messaging. Short Message Service, or SMS, had been used since the 1980s to send messages of up to 160 characters to phones, pagers, and other mobile devices. To help people send and receive text messages, cell phone companies developed "short codes," numbers with fewer digits than a regular telephone number.

Although Jack was often the first person in the room to know about new technologies, he knew little about SMS messaging until a friend at Odeo told him that she used text messaging on her cell phone constantly. Jack was amazed by the way people were starting to use texting to quickly communicate with each other. He quickly realized that he could tie SMS messages to his idea of sharing up-to-the-minute personal news with friends.

After that famous playground brainstorming session, Jack told Biz and Ev about his idea. He later remembered how the Odeo team ran with it: "We all kind of went into a corner, wrote out a bunch of user scenarios, and started inviting co-workers in. They fell in love with it. We knew we had something."

Ev Williams later recalled how Jack explained his idea for what would become Twitter:

"He said, 'Look, I've got this idea. Think about a buddy list, AIM, look at the 10 or 12 people that you see on your list but just look at their status messages. You get a sense of what everyone's doing, even if they're just getting coffee or out sick or too busy to chat."

With Odeo's business future in big trouble, that "aha!" moment came just in time. It took about two weeks for the team at Odeo to program a Web site tied to SMS messaging that would let people post short messages, or "tweets." They set the length of tweets to no more than 140 characters. That was because SMS messages could be no more than 160 characters, and each tweet also needed to include the name of the person sending it—a person's unique Twitter name can be up to fifteen characters.

Jack and his fellow Odeo programmers wanted a name for the new status-updating service that would be short and easy to remember, like the photo-sharing service Flickr and other new online services.

They brainstormed and came up with names like Jitter and Twitch, Jack remembers. None of the names were very good at first. Why not call it "Friendstalker!" joked one person on the team.

Then, Odeo's Noah Glass went through the dictionary and found the word twitter, which means short, inconsequential bursts of information, or the chirps of birds.

Twitter sounded like a perfect name for the new product. But at first they shortened it to Twttr, so it would have five letters just as American text messaging short codes had five numbers. They hoped they could use the SMS "short code" equivalent of Twttr, 89887. But when they discovered that Teen People Magazine already owned that SMS number, Odeo added back the vowels and Twitter was the name from then on.

On March 21, 2006, at 12:50 p.m., Jack Dorsey celebrated his birthday and tested his new program by sending the message, "just setting up my twttr." It was just five words, but it was the start of something really big. One of the first messages Stone sent to Dorsey mimicked the words of the inventor Alexander Graham Bell's pioneering telephone call: "Mr. Watson—come here—I want to see you."

The Detroit News Timely Topics

Bell's First Telephone   UNDERWOOD & UNDERWOOD, INC.

Alexander Graham Bell's telephone

In July, they launched the Twitter.com Web site, and a few members of the public began to try it. Some loved it right away. Others didn't get the idea, or even hated it. One person, commenting about an online review of Twitter.com, called the service "the dumbest thing ever!" and wondered why anyone would put their personal activities on a Web site for anyone to see.

But enough people liked the idea that the programmers at Odeo believed it was time to leave podcasting behind and focus completely on Twitter. In October 2006, they started a separate company, which they named Obvious, and bought the rights to Twitter.com from Odeo's investors.

Jack's idea for people to constantly share where they were and what they were doing was finally out in the open, but would it succeed, or would it die like his childhood courier business or like dNET, his first California business? Since people weren't paying to use Twitter.com, how would the new company make money? For the rest of 2006, nobody knew the answers to those questions. 2007 would change everything.

er: What are you doing?

ɜwitter

An early version of Twitter's Web site in 2008

Chapter 4

What is Twitter?

Building the Buzz

By early 2007, people were using Twitter to send a few thousand tweets a day. It was promising, but not enough to guarantee business success. Jack, Ev, and Biz needed to get enough influential people to use their service, to start the "buzz" that would get the public to pay attention—and get investors to pay money to build the company.

In March that year, the team set up large plasma computer monitors in the hallway at the South by Southwest festival, also known as SXSW, an annual event in Austin, Texas, that features new ideas in music, film, and technology. On the display screens, people at the conference could see a constant stream of tweets about what people at the festival were saying and doing. Attendees started pulling out their cell phones to send text messages so they could see their comments on the big screens too.

Pete Townshend of the band The Who acts out playing the guitar during his keynote speech at the South by Southwest Music Festival in Austin, Texas, in 2007.

The promotional idea paid off quickly: Twitter messages tripled during the 2007 SXSW event. Speakers and bloggers at the festival started talking and writing—and tweeting, of course—about Twitter. When the event was over, many of those in attendance went back to their homes and jobs eager to continue using the new message service and tell their friends about it. The buzz was building.

At the same time, people outside the technology field were beginning to experiment with Twitter and other social media. Two U.S. senators, John Edwards—whose Twitter name was @johnedwards—and Barack Obama (@barackobama), signed up in early 2007 as they and their campaign staffers prepared to use it and other social media, including Facebook and MySpace, to connect with voters in the 2008 presidential campaign.

In April 2007, Obvious Corporation spun off Twitter into its own company, and made Jack Dorsey the CEO. Now, he had the responsibility to raise more venture capital from investors. He remembers that before he went to ask for big investments, he took out his nose ring. But as important as that part of the business became, Jack spent as much time as possible doing what he loved: improving the way Twitter worked.

The SXSW festival had brought Twitter to the attention of bloggers and other social media personalities. Politicians and a few other people were quietly testing it. But it would take a higher-profile "happening" to get

A marquee promoting the 2007 MTV Music Awards
outside the Palms hotel in Las Vegas

the public excited about using Twitter. That came along in September 2007, when the producers of the televised MTV Music Awards promoted live Twitter messages as a new way for fans to connect with their favorite music stars. The music network used the Twitter account @mtvmoonman to comment during the awards, and thousands of MTV fans responded by signing up for Twitter.

Now, Twitter was getting attention from everywhere it seemed. Once again, however, all of the attention wasn't positive. Some writers and comedians poked fun at Twitter users for sending messages about what they were eating for breakfast—and whether it tasted good or not. To some, it seemed like Twitter was just another sign that Americans were shallow and lazy. But "microblogging," as Twitter was sometimes called, was steadily gaining in popularity for more serious use too.

As the 2008 election approached, both Barack Obama and John McCain used Twitter to give updates about their campaign schedules and views on political issues. Twitter use jumped during the party nomination acceptance speeches for both candidates, a sign that tweets would fly fast and furious until the election. They did.

Twitter surged even more as the candidates and their vice presidential running mates, Sarah Palin and Joe Biden, conducted a series of debates. As the public warmed to following news and opinions on Twitter, the company even created a special page on Twitter.com that showed only tweets related to the election.

As the competition between candidates heated up across the United States in late 2008, another competition developed inside Twitter. Although Jack had successfully raised money for the company twice since its launch in 2007, he and Ev Williams didn't always agree on how the business should be run. In September 2008, the company's board of directors settled the debate by replacing Jack with Ev as CEO. Jack was made chairman of the company. It was an important position, but he later said that when he was removed as CEO "It felt like being punched in the stomach."

And yet Jack realized that Twitter's success was still not a sure thing. The rapid growth of the service was both good and bad. Users began to complain about frequent crashes as Twitter became overwhelmed with millions of messages. And the investors that Jack had convinced to provide more money were constantly asking how and when Twitter was going to begin making money on its own. Would they charge people or companies for using Twitter? Would they sell ads? Or would Twitter make money some other way?

If Twitter employees thought it was hard to keep the system running during the first few months of the presidential campaign, the month of November showed them they hadn't seen anything yet. On Election Day, as television news viewers turned to the Internet for the latest information on voting results, something amazing happened: in one day, there was a 40 percent jump in new Twitter.com registrations. To add to demand, later that same month NBA star Shaquille O'Neal joined a growing number of sports and entertainment celebrities on Twitter. He brought with him a huge number of new Twitter subscribers eager to hear the latest words from Shaq—whose short, often funny, comments to the media seemed a perfect match for the microblogging limits of Twitter.

By the end of 2008, Twitter was averaging 100 million tweets every three months. One of those messages, a private, or direct message, in November, was believed to be the one billionth tweet sent on Twitter. Considering it had been less than three years since Jack Dorsey first tweeted, "just setting up my twttr," that billionth message came amazingly fast.

The Internet Grows Up

In the twenty-first century, it's hard to imagine a time when the Internet wasn't available. But the Internet that people now take for granted has existed only since the early 1990s.

Before that, scientists and other researchers in the 1960s used a computer network known as ARPANET to send information to each other. The U.S. military and colleges had invented that design for safely connecting computers to each other. At first, those were the only places that had any use for that kind of networking.

There were no such things as Google, iTunes, or World of Warcraft. Believe it or not, the computer games of the time were text games: you played them by reading a description of a room or situation, and then typed instructions, such as "pick up the sword." It wasn't flashy, but it was exciting at the time.

Then in the 1970s and 1980s powerful new networks were built to connect computers in Europe, North America, Australia, and Asia. Businesses realized that they could use computer networks to communicate with each other and with their customers. By the late 1980s— around the time that Germans began to tear down the Berlin Wall, and the United States and Soviet Union moved to end the Cold War—new ways of using computer networks were seen worldwide.

At that point, e-mail and other communication on the Internet was still pretty basic: numbers and letters. No pictures or sound.

But in 1989 the English computer scientist Tim Berners-Lee came up with the idea for a World Wide Web, a way that anyone could use a computer to share words, pictures, and other information with someone else on the Internet. It didn't take long before "www" became the most famous three letters in the world. The Internet was growing rapidly at the same time that young Jack Dorsey was using his dad's computer to learn programming and imagine all the possibilities.

By the early 2000s, the computer network that had started as a way for Army and college engineers to work turned into a place where people could buy things, check their bank accounts, attend a college class, and, yes, post their latest news on Twitter, Facebook, or other social networks. The Internet was much more than a hobby for computer nerds. It was becoming the way millions of people live their lives.

Chapter 5

What is Twitter?

A Plane in the Hudson

In 2009, the fact that Twitter had needed to create a "buzz" three years earlier seemed almost hard to imagine. Now, the public attention to Twitter was more like a roar. From nearly every corner of American society, new ways of using tweets appeared, along with demands for new features and more reliable Twitter service.

It didn't take long for a dramatic news event to show that Twitter was being used for more than saying what kind of cereal people were eating. On January 15, 2009, a

US Airways flight ran into a flock of birds during takeoff from New York's LaGuardia Airport. Within minutes, the plane had lost power in its engines and its pilot, "Sully" Sullenberger, began looking for a way to land the plane in the middle of New York City, in the middle of a weekday afternoon. His chosen landing spot in that desperate situation was the middle of the Hudson River. Amazingly, Sullenberger landed the damaged airliner in the water with more than 150 passengers and crew aboard. All survived, were evacuated by crew members onto the wings of the plane, and were soon rescued from the sinking plane by responding ferry boats and other craft.

As local and national news organizations scrambled to send news crews to cover the drama on the Hudson, a Twitter user, Janis Krums (@jkrums), got there first. And his Twitter followers—and millions of others on Twitter—first got the news from him rather than on TV. A passenger on one of the ferries that

Airline passengers wait to be rescued on the wings of a US Airways jetliner that safely landed in the Hudson River in New York after a flock of birds knocked out both of its engines.

changed course to respond to the crash landing, Krums used his phone to take a picture of the US Airways jet in the water, its wings crowded with people. He posted the photo using Twitter's TwitPic feature, and tweeted the now-famous words, "There's a plane in the Hudson. I'm on the ferry going to pick up the people. Crazy."

Although it was just a case of a Twitter user being in the right place and time to snap a photo and post it online, the event sparked widespread discussion about how people were beginning to use Twitter not just to say what they were doing, but also to share news and information.

The Twitter trio has always said that many of the best improvements in Twitter came from the ideas of ordinary people using the service, not from programmers at the company. They decided from the beginning to encourage those ideas, a strategy that helped keep Twitter popular even when the company was struggling to keep its Web site running under the strain of millions of messages.

In 2009, Twitter put several of those ideas into production. One of the most important was the ability to search by keywords for what people were tweeting. Without public searching capability, Twitter users had only been able to read the updates of people they followed, or of a celebrity or other person whose Twitter name they knew. Now, anyone could search Twitter messages much as they search the rest of the Internet using Google or other search engines.

Twitter users often saw a tweet they wanted to respond to, or share with other people. So they came up with creative ways to do those things too. To reply to a tweet by someone, they would begin a new tweet with the @ symbol and the original tweeter's name, and follow it with a comment or answer. To show other people what someone else had tweeted, they began to use the letters RT, which stood for re-tweet, followed by the name of the original tweeter and original message. Now, everyone following the second person's Twitter feed could see what had been posted by another person, whether they followed the original tweeter or not. It became the Twitter version of the same kind of word-of-mouth communication that people have used for centuries to spread information to their friends and neighbors.

At Twitter, the programmers sometimes were amazed by the creativity of their subscribers. And they responded. Since people clearly wanted to know what was being talked about on a given day on Twitter, the service introduced "trending topics," a list of ten subjects or words that were being used the most by people all over the world. Someone even figured out a way to show a map of the world on the Internet that displayed tweets a few seconds after they were posted by individuals in South America, Asia, Africa, Australia, Europe, and North America. Twittervision, as it was called, was a creative example of an Internet "mashup," any Web page or program that

A screen shot shows a Twitter user's location after they've tweeted.

combines data from two or more unrelated sources to create an entirely new information resource. Twittervision's inventor programmed it to take the public Twitter feed—an open timeline of tweets from anyone—and use the location information provided by the Twitter users' profiles to display the tweets on a map of the world created from Google Maps. As a new tweet was displayed from someone in Beijing, China, the Twittervision map would rotate so China was in the center of the screen. Then a tweet from someone in Atlanta or Los Angeles would cause the map to spin toward North America.

It was just one of hundreds of third-party applications—programs created by people outside Twitter—that exposed Twitter to a much larger audience than it might have had only on its own Web site. Twitter allowed companies that followed certain guidelines to use technical information about Twitter's application programming interface, or API, and create new ways of using Twitter on computers, cell phones, and other gadgets. Some of those programs became so popular that millions of Twitter subscribers rarely visited Twitter.com directly. That was OK with Jack, Ev, and Biz, as long as more people got involved with Twitter.

By mid-2009, with many celebrities and public figures using Twitter—and some of them worried about having their names used on Twitter without their permission—the service came out with verified accounts. Now, people who saw tweets by someone claiming to be Oprah

Winfrey or Barack Obama could see at a glance whether Twitter had confirmed the account was actually being used by that famous person. Celebrities, whose names are a valuable business asset, had a little more control over how their names were used online.

For a service that started with only Jack and five co-workers "following" each other's Twitter messages, it was amazing that some Twitter accounts were now being followed by thousands—even hundreds of thousands—of people. It was only a matter of time, it seemed, until somebody would have a million followers. The "race" to get one million followers took on a life of its own and drew even more news media attention to Twitter. Actor Ashton Kutcher's fun-loving personality and big fan base

Ashton Kutcher, left, with Jack Dorsey at the U.S. Innovation Delegation press conference in Moscow in 2010

quickly built his Twitter account, @asplusk, into one of the most popular. He and Jack Dorsey became friends after meeting because of Twitter.

A British programmer, James Cox, had started the Twitter account @cnnbrk in 2007 to post tweets about whatever he saw happening on the CNN television network. The account became widely popular on Twitter, and the network even hired Cox to continue posting with their permission on @cnnbrk. Then, in 2009, CNN bought the popular account from him and worked to attract even more followers. Suddenly, it became clear that CNN and Ashton Kutcher were approaching 1 million followers. Fans of both accounts encouraged their friends on Twitter to help their favorite account get there first. Some people even signed up for Twitter for the first time just to see what the race was all about and add their "vote."

At just after 2 a.m. in the morning Eastern time on April 17, 2009, the actor beat the news network to a million followers. About thirty minutes later, CNN's Twitter account passed 1 million too. It seemed like a lot of followers then, but just two years later, Kutcher had more than 6 million followers, and the original CNN account more than 4 million.

Although the lives of famous people were drawing more attention every day on Twitter, it was the death of a celebrity that brought the service—and several Internet news sites—to a standstill. When pop superstar Michael Jackson died June 25, 2009, people posted hundreds of thousands of tweets within the first few minutes of hearing the news. Rumors first flew about whether the singer was alive or not, and then turned to an outpouring of grief and tributes as the news of his death was confirmed.

Twitter servers strained to keep up, ran more than twenty minutes behind in displaying tweets, and even stopped working temporarily, before technicians were able to restore normal service. Within the twelve months from mid-2008 to mid-2009, the effect of major events such as a presidential election, a plane crash in New York, and a celebrity's death had driven countless new users to Twitter and tested the ability of the company's workers to keep the service running.

Now, they had to find a way to turn the popularity of Twitter into profitability for investors. By the end of the year, some business analysts estimated that Twitter was worth approximately $1 billion. The trick would be finding ways to produce revenue without losing the hundreds of thousands of new Twitter subscribers who were accustomed to using Twitter for free.

follow ash

twit

LAM

A digital billboard in Decatur, Illinois, with the message "follow ashton kutcher" promotes the competition between Kutcher and CNN in 2009.

Key Twitter Terms

Most people find that using Twitter is fairly easy, with only a few basic terms and techniques required. The team that developed Twitter designed it that way, so the service could be used on a wide variety of devices, from cell phones to computers. Here are some key Twitter terms:

///////// **User name:** A person's Twitter name, or "handle," as it is also known, can be up to fifteen characters, and has to be different from anyone else using Twitter. Jack Dorsey is @jack, Evan Williams is @ev, and Biz Stone is @biz.

///////// **Tweet:** the noun for a message on Twitter, or the verb meaning to post a message.

///////// **Direct message:** Known as a DM for short, this is a private message sent by one Twitter user to another user, rather than tweeted for all followers to see. You can only DM someone if they follow you on Twitter.

///////// **Hashtag:** Invented by Twitter users, hashtags are a word or phrase preceded by the # sign, or hash mark. They are a way to let other people easily search for tweets posted on that subject by anyone regardless of whether they follow them or not. Right after the March 2011 earthquake and tsunami in Japan, for example, many Twitter users began including #japan or #tsunami in their tweets for easy searching.

///////// **Notifications:** Twitter users can set up their account to send them automatic e-mails or text messages for various reasons, such as getting a new follower or receiving a direct message. Some people use Twitter almost exclusively on their phones, while others use it on their computers or through a combination of the two technologies.

- **Mentions and replies:** If you include the @ symbol and a person's Twitter handle in a tweet, you are said to "mention" them on Twitter. Replies are a type of Mention: you click on the Reply button next to someone's tweet to answer something they tweeted.
- **Follow:** Subscribe to another Twitter user's tweets. To unsubscribe from those tweets, you select the "Unfollow" button next to the person's user name.
- **Follower:** someone who is following, or subscribing, to your tweets.
- **Retweet:** Copying and forwarding to others a tweet by someone else.
- **Lists:** Twitter users can set up lists of Twitter users so they can read the messages posted by people even if they don't follow them. People often use lists to organize Twitter users by categories of interest or subject matter. They also can share their lists with other people, who can subscribe to or "follow" those lists that appeal to them.
- **Timeline:** The real-time messages posted on Twitter. What's in your timeline can include many types of messages, including those posted by people you follow, replies to your own tweets, and retweets of your messages.
- **Trending Topics:** Twitter uses a complex program to analyze what people are posting at any given hour of the night or day. A current list of trending topics is displayed on a person's Twitter page, and they can click on the name of a topic to see messages anyone has posted about that topic in the last few seconds or hours. When Michael Jackson died in 2009, nine of the 10 trending topics that afternoon in the United States were related to him.

Chapter 6

New Twitter, New Challenges

With a billion tweets behind them by the end of 2009, the Twitter team wondered if things could possibly get any busier. In 2010, they did.

Early that year, Biz Stone tweeted, "Today we are celebrating our 140th employee at Twitter!" For a company that had begun with only a few people just four years before, it was quite an accomplishment to reach the symbolic number of employees equal to the maximum length of characters in a tweet. But they wouldn't get much time to sit around and celebrate.

Before long, people on Twitter were sending more than 50 million tweets every day. Some of those messages were out of the ordinary, to say the least. In fact, some were literally out of this world. On January 22, 2010, NASA astronaut T. J. Creamer posted the first unassisted tweet from space, where he was on assignment at the International Space Station. Before then, other NASA astronauts had posted on Twitter by relaying messages to technicians on the ground, who then sent the tweets, but Creamer's ISS tweet was the first time somebody not on planet Earth logged in to their Twitter account and posted a message.

NASA astronaut T. J. Creamer, front left, with the crews from the Space Shuttle Atlantis and the International Space Station on NASA TV

Sometimes, the person doing the tweeting is a bigger deal than the content of the tweet itself. That was certainly true in January 2010 when Microsoft founder and personal computing legend Bill Gates set up a verified Twitter account and posted his first message on the service. For Jack Dorsey, Ev Williams, Biz Stone, and the other members of the original Twitter team, the presence of Gates and other Silicon Valley heroes on their site was exciting. Within a year @BillGates had more than 2 million followers on Twitter. In 2011 he was using his Twitter account to promote the work done by his and his wife Melinda's foundation, which focuses on health and poverty issues around the world.

For Jack Dorsey, losing the CEO position at Twitter back in 2008 had given him time to work on other projects. It didn't take long for him to find something he thought had almost as much potential as Twitter. In 2009 he co-founded Square, a new company that let anyone with a smart phone accept credit card payments. One of his co-founders was Jack McKelvey, the man who had hired young Jack Dorsey as a summer intern in St. Louis. The name of their new company referred to a small plastic gadget that a person could plug into their mobile phone and then use to swipe a credit card.

The idea of small businesses taking credit cards wasn't new, but as the leader of Square, Jack was determined to make it easy for them to get paid anytime, anywhere. His lifelong interest in taxis and package couriers hadn't just been about where they were on the map and where they were going. It was also important to know how those drivers and delivery people got paid for what they did. Before dNET had failed, he and Greg Kidd had envisioned an online dispatch Web site that included a way to pay couriers. Square, Jack realized, would have a chance to make on-the-spot payments easier for everyone, no matter what business they ran. He said:

> Payment is another form of communication but it's never been treated as such. It's never been designed. It's never felt magical. About 90 percent of Americans carry cards, but almost nobody can accept them. We want to balance that out and just make payments feel amazing.

With millions of small business owners using cell phones and nearly all of their customers used to using credit cards for everyday items, Jack thought Square had big potential. So did several venture capital investors. Once again, Jack's big ideas were able to attract big money, to the tune of $10 million in 2009 and more than twice that amount in early 2011. By then, the company based on a square piece of plastic and Jack Dorsey's idea was thought to be worth more than $240 million.

As always, at Square, Jack believed that the important thing in business was to respect ideas, and be ready for

Jim McKelvey presents the Square, a new electronic payment system developed by Jack Dorsey.

them regardless of who thought of them or what time they happened. Ideas, he said, "can come from anyone, and they can come anytime. We all have various directions that we want to take the company and sometimes those ideas come during a shower, sometimes they come when we're walking, sometimes they come when we're talking with other employees at the coffee store."

But while Jack and his new co-workers were busy building their ideas at Square into another business success, his thoughts were never far away from Twitter. He believed the two companies both had big futures.

"I think Twitter is the future of communications and Square will be the payment network. We're going big," Jack said.

As Twitter continued to grow in 2010, the company decided it was time to launch a new version of the site. On September 14, 2010, the new Twitter.com went live, along with a new Twitter logo. Some of the features added to the new version of the site were similar to popular features of programs like TweetDeck and Seesmic Desktop that other companies had created to make Twitter easier to use. In addition, the new version of Twitter made it easier for people to share and view pictures, video, and other multimedia content. The simple SMS-based message service that Jack Dorsey and friends had launched in 2006 was all grown up now.

But with all the new features and millions of new followers, Twitter also attracted trouble in the form of computer viruses. Only a week after the new version was launched, a sophisticated virus appeared that affected PC-based Twitter users even if they didn't click on a link in a tweet, but only pointed their mouse cursor at a tweet. The virus temporarily hijacked many Twitter users' accounts and caused an uproar among them and millions of other subscribers who were already adjusting to the new look of Twitter.com.

But Twitter survived this and other short-term problems and continued to grow rapidly in late 2010.

The challenges and yet another round of demands from investors, however, caused another change in leadership at Twitter. Ev Williams, who had replaced Jack Dorsey as CEO two years before, stepped down in October 2010 and was replaced as CEO by Dick Costolo. Ev stayed with Twitter to focus on the strategy for the service.

The Fail Whale

Sometimes, a high volume of tweets in a short period of time—such as a major news event—causes Twitter to be unable to display users' timelines. In that case, a message pops up saying that "Twitter is over capacity," accompanied by a now-famous cartoon drawing of a whale being lifted in the air by strings pulled by a flock of birds that look something like the bird in the Twitter logo. This image, an illustration by designer Yiying Lu, was picked by Twitter to symbolize the hard work of technicians who were working to fix the temporary Twitter outage. But Twitter users started calling it the "Fail Whale" to express their frustration with the problems. As always, the developers at Twitter learned to go along with their loyal subscribers, still calling it the Over Capacity error message but acknowledging that it's also the Fail Whale.

The designer Lu originally drew the image as a happy message to some of her friends overseas, but she has become used to its Twitter meaning too. She said:

> The original icon and symbolism was originally about good wishes and happy thoughts, and that's what this image is all about. And I guess that's why people really love it. … Rather than people seeing the picture as a sign of technology's failure, they should see it as a sign of, you know, 'sit back and relax.'

twitter

Home ›

Twitter is over capacity.

Please wait a moment and try again. For more information, check out Twitter Status »

© 2010 Twitter   About Us   Contact   Blog   Status   API   Help   Jobs   TOS   Privacy

twitter

Chapter 7

What is Twitter?

Twitter 'Round the World

The success of Twitter gave Jack Dorsey a chance to travel all over the world to promote the service and talk with people about how they were using it. In 2009, in an interview with Agoranews in Europe, he talked about one potential effect of Twitter: "I'm really excited about what technologies like this can do for government and getting more of the citizens engaged into public action and public policy and into that conversation of how we structure our societies, how we structure our cultures, and what we want to see in the world."

What actually happened on Twitter around the world in 2009 definitely got many citizens involved, but some of their governments weren't very happy about it. In April, the government in China blocked access to Twitter and many other online social media sites in order to limit unapproved communication by Chinese people about the anniversary of the Tiananmen Square protests of 1989, also known as the Tiananmen Square massacre. An unknown number of people demonstrating for greater political freedom were killed by the Chinese army in April 1989, and news images from the event had been watched worldwide.

In April 2009 a country far to the west of China wasn't as prepared to block Twitter communication by protesters. Several thousand young people rioted against the Communist leaders and the outcome of an election in Moldova, an Eastern European country formed in 1991 when the Soviet Union dissolved. Some of the protesters posted news on Twitter about what was happening in the streets. They even created a hashtag, #pman, designed to let people in Moldova and around the world follow the fast-moving events.

In June 2009, unrest after another country's election also got attention on Twitter. Some people in Iran, who were angry about what they thought was a bogus election, took to the streets—and to Twitter—to demand reforms. Some people referred to this as the

People throw uniforms into a fire during a violent protest outside the parliament in Chisinau, Moldova, on April 7, 2009. Thousands of demonstrators denouncing a Communist victory in ex-Soviet Moldova's parliamentary election smashed windows of the president's offices and hurled stones at police.

"Twitter Revolution." Many Twitter users around the world even changed the color or content of their Twitter profile pictures temporarily to show solidarity with the people of Iran.

When Iran's government responded to the trouble by blocking text messages and the ability of foreign news media to send pictures and video outside the country, many Iranians filled the gap by posting thousands of updates on Twitter via the Internet. Jack Dorsey even got an urgent e-mail from the U.S. State Department during the crisis. Twitter had been planning a short outage of Twitter.com to update the service, but U.S. diplomats hoped Twitter would delay the outage so the Iranian demonstrators would have a way to communicate. They told Jack, "It appears Twitter is playing an important role at a crucial time in Iran. Could you keep it going?" Jack contacted the team at Twitter, who delayed the outage.

In the end, the protests in Moldova and Iran failed to change the outcome of those elections. But the use of Twitter was growing among people living in societies where the regular news media was controlled by their governments. Because Twitter could be used by anyone with a cell phone, it was an option for political protest even when regular Internet access was blocked.

Other dramatic political events would soon play out on Twitter around the world. But all of the tweets weren't about life-and-death struggles. The 2010 World Cup, soccer's world championship held every four years, was the first such event held after Twitter became widely known outside the United States. The results were astonishing. During several weeks leading up to the final match in South Africa, in which Spain defeated the Netherlands, millions of fans around the world tweeted constantly about their teams and their matches.

World Cup activity turned into the biggest event until that time on Twitter, although by the end of 2010 the BP oil spill in the Gulf of Mexico created even more tweets. During the last minutes of the World Cup final, there were more than 2,000 tweets per second on Twitter. And it wasn't just people in Spain and the Netherlands doing the tweeting. During the match, people from more than 170 countries posted tweets in twenty-seven languages. There were more than 3,000 tweets per second, coming from more than eighty nations, in the minutes right after Spain's winning goal.

Spain's Andres Iniesta celebrates winning the 2010 World Cup as the final whistle is blown.

Jack Dorsey's vision for Twitter was coming true. But even bigger things were still to come. Jack had told anyone who wanted to talk about Twitter that the service at its best was just another tool for conversation:

> My favorite aspect of Twitter is when it sparks interaction, face-to-face interaction, when it sparks conversation. I love seeing that people are getting together and using this as a spark and then talking about their lives. Not talking about Twitter but talking about what's important to them.

In late 2010 and early 2011, social media including Twitter played a role in a series of political upheavals in the Mideast. In Tunisia, unrest against a repressive government caused an uprising, known as the Jasmine Revolution, and caused the nation's dictator to leave the country. In Egypt, the world watched anxiously as a tense struggle developed in Cairo between people demanding democratic reforms and the government of Hosni Mubarak. In the end, Mubarak resigned. Within weeks, the wave of political unrest in the region spread to Bahrain, Yemen, Algeria, Iraq, and Libya. The degree of public protest in those countries ranged from public demonstrations in some cities to outright civil war in the case of Libya. But each time, citizens of those nations took to Twitter and other social networks to tell their side of the story. In every one of those upheavals, individuals, opposition political groups, and interested people around the globe checked Twitter for up-to-the-minute updates. Tweets came in 24/7, sometimes linking to cell phone photos and video of news as it happened.

Even before those political upheavals, Ev Williams described the power of Twitter's instant communication:

> Twitter lets people share moments of their lives whenever they want, be they momentous occasions or mundane ones. It's sharing these moments as they're happening that lets people feel more connected and in touch despite distance and in the real time. This is the primary use of Twitter we saw from the beginning and what got us excited. What we didn't anticipate was the many, many other uses that would evolve from this very simple system. This trend of people using this communication network to help each other out goes far beyond the original idea of just keeping up with family and friends. It seems like when you give people easier ways to share information, more good things happen. I have no idea what will happen next with Twitter, but I've learned to follow the hunch but never assume where it will go.

Twitter and world events

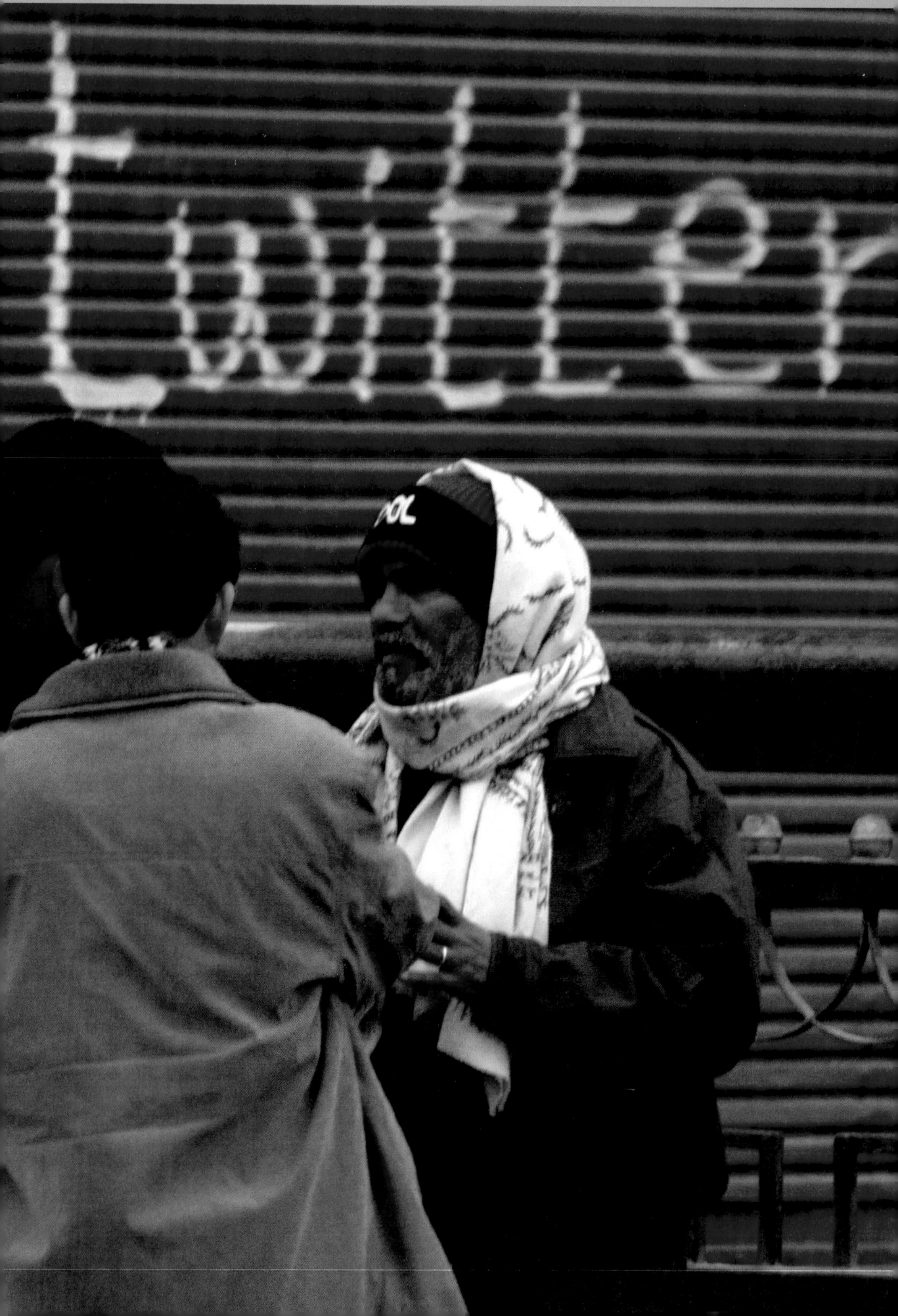

When Jack Dorsey posted the first-ever tweet in 2006, "just setting up my twttr," he could not have imagined how big a role his small messaging project would one day play in world events. He wouldn't have been completely surprised, considering the things Jack had learned about the power of information even when he was young.

Today, in a street protest in a country far away, some people may be throwing rocks, but Twitter messages are probably flying fast and furious too.

In some ways, the chaotic scenes from Cairo, Egypt, and several other cities in 2011 looked a lot like anti-government protests decades or even centuries ago: barricades, handwritten banners, enthusiastic chanting, and hand-to-hand fighting between people on different sides. But in Egypt—just as in Tunisia, Iran, Libya, Moldova, and other countries experiencing political unrest—Twitter, Facebook, and other Internet-based social networking sites have been there in the thick of things too.

Although it's hard to know how big a role the Internet has played in the unrest, one clue is how often the governments involved try to block Twitter and other messages, or just shut down Internet access completely.

Opposition supporters talk near graffiti referring to Twitter in Tahrir Square in Cairo in February 2011.

twitter

Chapter 8

What is Twitter?

Staying Connected

In March 2011, as Twitter reached its fifth birthday, the company published some statistics that showed how the service had grown. Although it had taken Twitter a little over three years to reach a total of 1 billion tweets, by early 2011 people were sending that many tweets every week. They were tweeting 140 million messages a day and the rate was growing almost faster than anyone could count.

People worldwide were signing up for Twitter at a dizzying pace, at a rate of nearly half a million new accounts every day. Then, news of a devastating March 11 earthquake and tsunami in Japan caused that number to jump even higher, with 572,000 new Twitter accounts opened on the following day alone. To keep up with demand, Twitter employed more than four hundred people by that time.

An upended house is among debris in Ofunato, Japan, following a 9.0 magnitude earthquake and subsequent tsunami in 2011.

Twitter was still owned by its private investors in early 2011, but analysts estimated the company was worth more than $4 billion. There were frequent rumors that a big company such as Google or Facebook was planning to buy Twitter. In some cases, people guessed that the purchase price would be $8 billion to $10 billion.

Through it all, the partners at Twitter tried to stay focused on keeping the service reliable and on listening to what Twitter subscribers wanted. Some people were complaining that Twitter was becoming too complicated and that it was becoming cluttered with advertisements. Then, just after Twitter's fifth birthday in late March 2011, the company answered the critics with a surprise announcement: Jack was back in charge of product development at Twitter. In that important role, he would make sure the service was in good shape for whatever happened next. Ev Williams, who had led product development for several months since stepping down as CEO, would no longer have an active role at Twitter, although he remained a big investor and a member of the company's board of directors.

Jack, who had suffered the shock of being replaced by Ev as CEO when Twitter was just taking off in 2008, was happy to be back in control of the idea he had helped turn into a success. But he said the return to Twitter wasn't the end of his work at Square. He tweeted, "Today I'm thrilled to get back to work at @Twitter leading product as executive chairman. And yes: leading @Square forevermore as C.E.O."

twitter

The best way to discover what's new

Gucci Mane   Raimundos   STOP STRESSING   Bloc

See who's here

Friends and industry peers you know. Celebrities you watch. Businesses you frequent. Find them all on Twitter.

Top Tw

R
in
sk

2

ep
m
an

2

th
ru
sk

in your wo

Libel Kate Hud

ets   View all ›

lTroyBrown80 Is it pos
rview about another player,
uld be more professional!

rs ago ·

licesupply Have you seen our Family Badges? Th
iature custom badges manufactured with the same car
workmanship... http://fb.me/OVLMvzkQ

rs ago ·

RealKiyosaki True leaders must make the rules, change the
s, and enforce the rules. Rules will test your leadership
s.

A 2011 screen shot of the Twitter Web site

How had Twitter gone from an idea in Jack Dorsey's mind to become one of the fastest-growing American businesses in history, and a technology affecting the lives of countless millions of people around the world? For Jack, it wasn't because he, Ev, Biz, and others at Twitter knew how to write fancy computer code or how to raise money from investors. It was because Twitter filled a basic need people have to communicate with people they know. He once explained it this way:

> When I first started developing Twitter, I wasn't really thinking about the usages beyond just keeping in constant connection with my friends. I think it's important when you first start something out that you have a focus like that, you have something that you really want to see in the world … because that really drives the work. But now, people are using it in ways we had no idea they would be using it for, and that's exciting to us.

In fact, he said, it didn't surprise him that Twitter was a success, just how fast it grew. Even when there were only five people at Odeo testing the new Twitter in 2006, they all knew they had something big. But, he admitted: "The surprising part is how quickly and immediate the service is becoming useful to millions of people. It is a bit scary but it's extremely exciting at the same time to have all of these people being able to act and interact in a very immediate way all over the world."

He got an early clue that people would do more with Twitter than say what they were thinking. Just after the ground shook from a minor earthquake in San Francisco, Jack checked his cell phone and saw a quick Twitter message from a friend asking, "was that an earthquake?" Within seconds, another of his Twitter friends said yes, and wondered how strong the quake had registered. Right after that, someone tweeted that the Web site of the U.S. Geological Service had confirmed it was an earthquake. That person also tweeted the initial USGS measurement of the power of the earthquake.

One technology expert has explained why Twitter is popular by comparing how people use it and how they use Google. "If you're looking for interesting articles or sites devoted to Kobe Bryant, you search Google. If you're looking for interesting comments from your extended social network about the three-pointer Kobe just made 30 seconds ago, you go to Twitter."

But one of the best descriptions of how Twitter works, and a hint of why people like it, came during a 2008 interview of Jack Dorsey by Jason Pontin, the editor of *Technology Review*. The interview was conducted, not surprisingly, through Twitter messages:

@jason_pontin @jack Explain Twitter.

@jack @jason_pontin Twitter is a real-time repository of state for people, events, & things. A personal news wire of sorts.

@jason_pontin @jack I twitter every day. But whenever I explain it to people who've not, they are uncomprehending or angry. Why?

@jack @jason_pontin People have to discover value for themselves. Especially w/ something as simple & subtle as Twitter. It's what you make of it.

Millions of users of Twitter are now making of it whatever they think is best. The prospects for even more growth seem good.

Twitter's founders say they are not interested in selling their creation, and each remains remarkably low-key. Biz Stone and his wife, Olivia, have created a foundation to support education and conservation in California. They own a small house in Marin County, California, and lease their cars. Ev Williams and his wife, Sara Morishige Williams, live in the San Francisco Bay area and when Sara went into labor with their son in 2009, she tweeted about it while still in the hospital.

Jack Dorsey bought his first car in early 2011, and he starts each day by texting his mother. He says he'd like to be the mayor of New York City, calling it the ultimate chance to live out his goal of understanding everything about how cities work. He even talked with Mayor Michael Bloomberg in 2010 about that idea; Bloomberg advised him to first make as much money as possible so he could afford to campaign someday.

No matter how Twitter may grow, any history of the twenty-first century will list the trio of Jack Dorsey, Evan Williams, and Biz Stone among a handful of entrepreneurs who transformed how people communicate.

twitter

What are you doing?

Going to |

TIMELINE

1972   Evan Williams born on March 31 in Clarks, Nebraska.

1974   Isaac "Biz" Stone born on March 10 in Boston, Massachusetts.

1976   Jack Dorsey born on November 19 in St. Louis, Missouri.

2004   Evan Williams co-founds the podcasting company, Odeo; Biz Stone moves from the East Coast to the West Coast to join Williams.

2005   Jack Dorsey joins Odeo.

2006   During a brainstorming session, Jack reveals his idea of using cell phone text messages to broadcast a person's current status to a group of people; on March 21, he posts the first Twitter message: "just setting up my twttr;" on July 13, Twitter.com goes live.

2007   Jack becomes CEO of Twitter; the same month, then Senator Barack Obama, posts his first tweet.

2008   Jack becomes chairman of Twitter, and Evan Williams takes over day-to-day operations as CEO; averaging 100 million tweets per quarter for the year, Twitter sees a 40 percent jump in signups on U.S. Election Day; the same month, a private message becomes the one billionth tweet, and NBA star Shaquille O'Neal's huge fan base follows him to Twitter.

2009   In response to Twitter subscriber ideas, the company adds searches, trending topics, verified accounts for celebrities, and other improvements; Twitter is rumored to be valued at more than $1 billion.

2010   Twitter passes 50 million tweets per day, including the first by Microsoft founder Bill Gates and the first tweet from the International Space Station; Evan Williams steps down as CEO of Twitter.

2011   As some reports value Twitter's business at $8 billion or more, the service provides value as a communication lifeline to members of opposition groups in several Muslim countries; as Twitter turns five years old, Jack Dorsey returns to lead product development.

SOURCES

Chapter One: The Magic of Maps

p. 11, "I was lucky enough . . ." Dom Sagolla, "How Twitter Was Born," *140 Characters*, January 20, 2009, www.140characters.com/2009/01/30/how-twitter-was-born/.

p. 12, "The first version . . ." Ibid.

p. 12, "Twitter is the side project . . ." Michael S. Malone, "The Twitter Revolution," *Wall Street Journal,* April 18, 2009.

p. 15, "Since I was very small . . ." Jeffrey Bussgang, "When Jack Dorsey Met Fred Wilson, And Other Twitter Tales (Excerpt from Mastering the VC Game)," TechCrunch.com, April 27, 2010.

p. 15, "was really creative . . ." Fran Mannino, "Twitter co-founder Jack Dorsey once lived in Affton," *South County Times*, September 11, 2009, http://www.southcountytimes.com/twitter.9.11.html.

p. 16, "My son loves computers," David Kirkpatrick, "Twitter Was Act One," *Vanity Fair*, April 2011.

p. 16, "I'll be with you . . ." Ibid.

p. 16, "Jack was exactly . . ." Ibid.

p. 17, "Just do everything . . ." Ibid.

p. 17, "I was the president of the company . . ." Tim Barker, "Native son sets St. Louis atwitter 'He's always seen life a little differently,' uncle says of Twitter creator," *St. Louis Post-Dispatch*, November 15, 2009, http://www.stltoday.com/news/article_635e1f22-b802-50d4-bc42-29a464ef72ad.html.

Chapter Two: East Coast, West Coast

p. 23, "90 miles . . ." Claire Cain Miller, "Why Twitter's C.E.O. Demoted Himself," *New York Times*, October 30, 2010.

p. 23, "a fierce desire . . ." Ibid.

p. 24, "I felt college . . ." Evan Williams, "For Twitter C.E.O., Well-Orchestrated Accidents," *New York Times*, March 8, 2009.

p. 25, "I had no business . . ." Ibid.

p. 25, "I was luck O'Reilly . . ." Evan Williams, "Going West, As a Young Man," EvHead (blog), November 1, 2007, http://evhead.com/2007/11/where-should-you-be.asp.

p. 26, "real relationship," Jonathan Guthrie, "Lunch with the FT: Biz Stone," *Financial* (London) *Times*, December 20, 2010.

p. 27,   "It turned out that . . ." Callum Borchers, "Twitter Co-Founder, Wellesley Native Biz Stone Addresses Babson Graduates," *Wellesley Patch*, May 15, 2011.

p. 27,   "Opportunity can be manufactured . . ." Ibid.

Chapter Three: Setting Up Twitter

p.36,   "I was fascinated with jeans . . ." Kirkpatrick, "Twitter Was Act One."

pp. 36-38,   "One night, I couldn't sleep . . ." Bussgang, "When Jack Dorsey Met Fred Wilson."

p. 38,   "I'm at the Bison Paddock . . ." Kevin Rose, "Twitter Interview with Jack Dorsey." Foundation 001, December 29, 2010, http://www.youtube.com/watch?v=DQy_HFHOZug.

p. 38,   "secondly, no one really . . ." Kirkpatrick, "Twitter Was Act One."

p. 41,   "We all kind of went . . ." Bussgang, "When Jack Dorsey Met Fred Wilson."

p. 42,   "He said, 'Look, I've got . . ." Andrew LaVallee, "Twitter Founders Talk About Its Origins, Next Steps and Social Alchemy," *Wall Street Journal: Digits*, May 27, 2009.

p. 42,   "Friendstalker!," Sagolla, "How Twitter Was Born."

p. 43,   "just setting up . . ." Dorsey, @jack Twitter feed.

p. 43,   "Mr. Watson . . ." Guthrie, "Lunch with the FT: Biz Stone."

Chapter Four: Building the Buzz

p. 52,   "It felt like . . ." Kirkpatrick, "Twitter Was Act One."

Chapter Five: A Plane in the Hudson

p. 60,   "There's a plane . . ." Janis Krums, @jkrums Twitter feed, January 15, 2009.

Chapter Six: New Twitter, New Challenges

p. 73,   "Today we are celebrating . . ." Biz Stone, @biz Twitter feed, February 16, 2010, http://twitter.com/#!/biz/status/9213048183.

p. 76,   "Payment is another form . . ." Kirkpatrick, "Twitter Was Act One."

p. 77,   "can come from anyone . . ." Erick Schonfeld, "Jack Dorsey & the Golden Gate Bridge," Transcript of speech at Square, TechCrunch.com, March 24, 2011.

p. 78,   "I think Twitter . . ." Kirkpatrick, "Twitter Was Act One."

p. 80,   "The original icon . . ." Zachary Sniderman, "The Origin of Twitter's "Fail Whale," Mashable.com, August 2, 2010.

Chapter Seven: Twitter 'Round the World

p. 83, "I'm really excited . . ." "A Video of Jack Dorsey, Founder and Chairman of Twitter" YouTube video, 3:46, from an interview selected by Vito Di Bari.com: Blogging the Future, http://www.youtube.com/watch?v=2w9RYpAmnOc.

p. 86, "It appears Twitter . . ." Mark Lander and Brian Stelter, "Washington Taps Into a Potent New Force in Diplomacy," *New York Times*, June 16, 2009, http://www.nytimes.com/2009/06/17/world/middleeast/17media.html.

p. 88, "My favorite aspect . . ." "A Video of Jack Dorsey, Founder and Chairman of Twitter" YouTube video.

p. 89, "Twitter lets people . . ." Evan Williams, "Evan Williams on Listening to Twitter Users," TED Talks, February 2009.

Chapter Eight: Staying Connected

p. 95, "Today I'm thrilled . . ." Dorsey, @jack Twitter timeline, http://twitter.com/#!/jack/status/52407042966695936.

p. 98, "When I first started . . ." Video interview of UNESCO Chair in E-learning in Barcelona, Spain, April 2, 2009.

p. 98-99, "The surprising part . . ." Ibid.

p. 99, "If you're looking . . ." Steven Johnson, "How Twitter Will Change the Way We Live," *Time*, June 5, 2009.

p. 100, "@jason_pontin @jack . . ." Jason Pontin, "2008 Young Innovators Under 35: Jack Dorsey, 31," *Technology Review*, September 2008, http://www.technologyreview.com/tr35/Profile.aspx?Cand=T&TRID=700.

BIBLIOGRAPHY

Barker, Tim Barker. "Native son sets St. Louis atwitter 'He's always seen life a little differently,' uncle says of Twitter creator." *St. Louis Post-Dispatch*, November 15, 2009. http://www.stltoday.com/news/article_635e1f22-b802-50d4-bc42-29a464ef72ad.html

Bussgang, Jeffrey. "When Jack Dorsey Met Fred Wilson, And Other Twitter Tales."April 27, 2010, TechCrunch.com.

Dorsey, Jack. @jack timeline. Twitter.com.

Johnson, Steven. "How Twitter Will Change the Way We Live." *Time*, June 5, 2009.

Kirkpatrick, David. "Twitter Was Act One." *Vanity Fair*, April 2011.

Lander, Mark, and Brian Stelter. "Washington Taps Into a Potent New Force in Diplomacy." *New York Times*, June 16, 2009. http://www.nytimes.com/2009/06/17/world/middleeast/17media.html.

LaVallee, Andrew. "Twitter Founders Talk About Its Origins, Next Steps and Social Alchemy." *Wall Street Journal: Digits*, May 27, 2009.

Lennon, Andrew, and Ella Keeven. "A Conversation With Twitter Co-Founder Jack Dorsey." *Daily Anchor*, February 12, 2009. http://www.thedailyanchor.com/2009/02/12/a-conversation-with-twitter-co-founder-jack-dorsey/.

Mannino, Fran. "Twitter co-founder Jack Dorsey once lived in Affton." *South County Times*, September 11, 2009. http://www.southcountytimes.com/twitter.9.11.html.

Pontin, Jason. "2008 Young Innovators Under 35: Jack Dorsey, 31." *Technology Review*, September 2008.

Rose, Kevin. "Twitter Interview with Jack Dorsey." Foundation 001, December 29, 2010. http://www.youtube.com/watch?v=DQy_HFHOZug.

Schonfeld, Erick. "Jack Dorsey & the Golden Gate Bridge." Transcript of speech at Square. TechCrunch.com, March 24, 2011.

http://techcrunch.com/2011/03/24/jack-dorsey-golden-gate-bridge/?utm_source=feedburner&utm_medium=feed&utm_campaign=Feed%3A+Techcrunch+%28TechCrunch%29.

Stone, Biz. @biz timeline. Twitter.com.

WEB SITES

http://www.twitter.com

The Official Web site of Twitter

http://www.the99percent.com/conference/speakers/jack_dorsey

On this site you'll find a video of Jack Dorsey talking about "The 3 Keys to Twitter's Success."

http:/www.vanityfair.com/business/features/2011/04/jack-dorsey-201104

Vanity Fair profile of Jack Dorsey

http://www.evhead.com

A blog by Evan Williams

http://www.ted.com/talks/evan_williams_on_listening_to_twitter_users.html

Video of Evan Williams on TED Talks

http://www.bizstone.com

Biz Stone's blog site

http://www.npr.org/ 2011/ 02/ 16/ 133775340/ twitters-biz-stone-on-starting-a-revolution

Listen to NPR's interview with Biz Stone, or read highlights of the interview. "Twitter's Biz Stone on Starting a Revolution" runs for thirty-eight minutes and forty-three seconds.

INDEX

PHOTO CREDITS